Original title:
Whispers of Watermelon

Copyright © 2025 Creative Arts Management OÜ
All rights reserved.

Author: Harrison Blake
ISBN HARDBACK: 978-1-80586-290-1
ISBN PAPERBACK: 978-1-80586-762-3

An Unraveling of Tropical Tastes

In the garden where fruits collide,
A belly flop of seeds and pride.
Juicy laughs spill on the floor,
As we munch and beg for more.

A slice of sunlight, pure delight,
Sticky fingers reaching for height.
The laughter echoes, sweet and bold,
A feast of stories, ripe and old.

The Silence Between Bites

Crunchy chews that make you pause,
Between bites, we laugh because.
Each seed a cannonball of fate,
Pits flying, oh, such a state!

Gobs of sweetness, can't resist,
A playful nibble, you get kissed.
Juice dribbles down to your chin,
That's the best game to begin!

Sunkissed Whirls in Pinks and Greens

Underneath the summer sun,
Chasing slices, oh what fun!
Spinning round in sticky bliss,
Who knew fruit could taste like this?

Bright pink swirls in every bite,
Giggles dance in pure delight.
With every munch, a giggleed cheer,
We play like kids, not a care here.

Beneath Layers of Refreshing Flesh

With a flick and twist, we dive deep,
Into layers of laughter we keep.
Seeds squirt like tiny surprise,
An explosion of joy that never dies!

Biting in, feeling so free,
Juicy jewels for you and me.
As we feast in this fruity land,
Life's a slice, let's take a stand.

Melodies from the Patch

In the patch, the fruit does dance,
Vines twirl round in a jolly prance.
Seeds are scattered, giggles abound,
Juicy tales in every sound.

Bouncing berries, bright and bold,
Green hats on, the stories told.
A picnic feast, with sun so bright,
Silly faces, such a sight!

Tales of the Orchard's Breath

Under trees, the laughter flows,
Round and round, the spinning grows.
Silly squirrels, they join the fun,
Chasing shadows, on the run.

A fruit fight breaks, with seeds a-fly,
Juicy smiles, oh my, oh my!
Drenched in joy, we gather near,
Picking fruit, and sharing cheer.

Beneath the Skin of Summer's Bliss

Sun-kissed skin, the laughter swells,
Fruit in hand, we hear the bells.
Ticklish bites, the taste so fine,
Giggles burst like fizzy wine.

A hundred shades of joyous spree,
Rolling hills, come play with me!
Whirlwind spins of sweet delight,
Warmth and chuckles, purest light.

Juiced Imaginations Amidst the Fields

Fields of laughter, ripe and great,
Dancing fruits can hardly wait.
Chubby cheeks and sticky hands,
Together we dream of far-off lands.

Lemonade lakes and berry boats,
Splashes of fun, as joy promotes.
Counting seeds, we share a chart,
Crafting gold from every heart.

Beneath the Green Canopy

Under leaves, a secret tune,
A juicy dance, from noon to moon.
With every bite, a giggle grows,
As sticky fingers play in rows.

Seeds fly like dreams in playful air,
Laughter spills in summer's stare.
Beneath the green, we find our glee,
While wedges wink so happily.

Fragrant Dreams of Summer Days

Bright slices gleam in sunlight's glow,
With sticky smiles, we steal the show.
   A pop of color, a burst of cheer,
  As carefree giggles fill the sphere.

Cool and sweet as a breeze on a fling,
We chase the joy that summers bring.
In a patch of bliss, the fun won't end,
We share each laugh, a summer friend.

The Hidden Essence of a Sliced Heart

A heart so red, with laughter packed,
Each vibrant slice, a silly act.
Juicy secrets slip around,
As giggles grow, they're safe and sound.

Cutting through, the joy cascades,
With every slice, the humor parades.
In every bite, a punchline waits,
As summertime always celebrates.

Nectar Dripping from Summer's Embrace

Sweet nectar drips from every edge,
Playing tricks like a cheeky pledge.
With each drop, a tickled grin,
In the warm sun, we spin and spin.

Happiness pools, a juicy jest,
Relishing summer's playful quest.
In every drop, a giggle flows,
As laughter blooms wherever we go.

Golden Hours in Green Enclosures

In fields where oddities abound,
Nibbles of laughter can be found.
Water's glisten, seeds on the run,
Who knew summer could be this fun?

A splash of juice, a squirty surprise,
As sticky fingers claim their prize.
Beneath the sun, we dance and leap,
In a patch where the giggles creep.

The Dance of Juicy Fare

Round and round, the fruit we spin,
A contest to see who gets the grin.
With bites like laughter, wild and free,
Each flavor a note in our jubilee.

Splat! A seed launches with flair,
Land right on Ro's wild hair.
We snicker and snort, the sweetest game,
Playing tag with this juicy fame.

Ripened Tales of Summer Sun

Sunkissed stories under the tree,
Chasing droplets, feeling so free.
Every chuckle, every happy cheer,
As the sun wraps us in its warm sphere.

With laughter erupting like fizz,
Each slice garners giggles and whiz.
We weave our dreams in shades of pink,
In a fruit patch that makes us think.

Nature's Sweetest Serenade

In a green oasis where secrets hum,
A symphony swells; the taste buds drum.
Chomp! Not a soul can resist,
In this can't-miss, sweetness bliss.

Grass stains and grins on a wild spree,
Squeezed laughter blends with the spree.
Dancing antics in twilight's glow,
As we relish the tales we sow.

Ribbons of Taste and Memory

In the garden, bright and round,
A fruit that's often found,
A jester in its juicy skin,
With laughter that it pulls within.

Slice it thick, let the juice flow,
Sticky fingers, don't you know?
A seed or two, oh what a game,
Spitting them out, who's to blame?

Under sun with friends in tow,
We giggle, time starts to slow,
The dribbles down your chin will stick,
A moment that's both sweet and slick.

As the day drifts into night,
Stars above are shining bright,
With every bite, our hearts just swell,
A taste we all know very well.

A Tapestry Woven with Flavor

A patch of green, so fresh and bold,
Each slice a story to be told,
The laughter bubbles, bright and loud,
Amidst the joyous, sun-kissed crowd.

From picnic blankets, unseen treasures,
Smiling faces, simple pleasures,
Fruits collide in flavors vast,
Each bite a giggle, shadows cast.

The cooler holds its chilly prize,
A bounty where the sweetness lies,
Stacked high, a mountain of delight,
With seeds that conquer in their flight.

With sticky joy, the hearts do sing,
A close-knit bond that summer brings,
Each taste a thread, we weave and share,
In laughter, love hangs in the air.

The Lure of Summer's Harvest

On a sunny day, oh what a treat,
The fruit parade, can't be beat,
Dancing seeds in the summer breeze,
Oh, how they tickle, oh, how they tease!

Juices flow, a playful spree,
Sticky to our toes and knee,
In a grand feast we dive so deep,
As nature's sweets make us giggle and leap!

A treasure hunt on tongue and cheek,
The laughter shared with every peak,
Oh daring fruit, you charm our hearts,
In your embrace, the fun just starts!

With every bite, a giggle flies,
Who knew such joy could meet our eyes?
In the warmth of the golden rays,
The harvest dances, wild and plays.

Rainbows in Every Bite

Bright green jackets, a party for the eyes,
Juicy treasures hide where the laughter lies.
Silly seeds dance in a sticky parade,
Every crunch a joke, each slice is well-played.

Giggle in the sun, let the seeds take flight,
Sticky fingers painting, oh what a sight!
Frosty juice drips down, a smile so wide,
Nature's confetti, with sweetness inside.

Whispered Tales of Summer's Bounty

In the garden, tales are spun,
Of summer's laughter and the sun's warm fun.
Slice by slice, stories unfold,
A symphony of flavor, a legend told.

Each dripping wedge, a giggle and cheer,
As friends gather 'round, summer's magic is near.
With every bite, the world feels light,
In this juicy kingdom, everything's right.

The Color of Sweetness

Dressed in pink robes, oh so divine,
Every sugary piece, a little sunshine.
Round and plump, it rolls with glee,
Nature's candy, let's celebrate, whee!

Sliced like laughter, everyone grins,
In this sugary ocean, nobody sins.
On plates it twirls, a dance so spry,
Sweetness in every bite, oh my, oh my!

Gathered with the Harvest

Squeezed in baskets, they giggle and cheer,
Round the picnic table, everyone's here.
Nature's party begins with a plop,
As juicy dribbles make bellies stop!

Little hands reach for the summer delight,
Sharing sweet bites, feeling just right.
Chasing the juice with laughter loud,
In this fruity feast, we're joyfully proud.

Ripe Melodies Beneath the Sun

Under the sun, the fruit does grin,
Laughter bursts from within its skin.
Juicy secrets spill on the floor,
Tickling taste buds, begging for more.

Bouncing seeds with a funny cheer,
They're doing the dance, oh so near!
Slicing one slice leads to a joke,
The laughter echoes, as we poke.

Crimson joys in a sticky race,
Spitting seeds like we're in a chase.
Mirthful moments, friends close by,
Giggles mingle as flavors fly.

In this feast, we're gleeful pests,
Taste the fun, leave out the rests.
Joyous bites that make us sing,
Life's a party, let's taste the fling.

Songs of the Ruby Flesh

Beneath the shade where shadows play,
A ruby fruit leads the way.
Chomping down with silly glee,
Each bite releases pure jubilee.

Sticky hands and smirking grins,
An orchestra of fruity sins.
Slurpy sounds, the juices flow,
In this silliness, we let go.

Jokes are shared between each slice,
"Why is it sweet? Ain't it nice!"
Laughter erupts in juicy bursts,
As we take turns slaking our thirsts.

Melodies of crunch fill the air,
Fruity tunes without a care.
Gobbling joy wrapped in the skin,
With each slice, the fun begins.

Liquid Light and Sweet Delight

Dripping sunshine, oh so bright,
Sipping nectar, pure delight.
Splashing colors, laughter flies,
Each drop a burst of sweet surprise.

Giggling kids with cups held high,
"Can we drink it all? Oh, my!"
Rivers run from every sip,
Fun and giggles, let it drip.

Competing laughs with every taste,
A fruity race, we're in no haste.
Mimicking sounds as roles we play,
Making magic in our way.

Chasing puddles on the floor,
Each splash a giggle, never a bore.
Liquid joy swirls all around,
In this sweetness, we are found.

The Unspoken Language of Juices

In silent bites, the fruit declares,
A code of laughter, who really cares?
Chewing softly, we laugh aloud,
Sticky fingers in the crowd.

The language of sweetness, no words need,
Every fruit slice plants a seed.
In this banquet of pure delight,
We share the giggles, day and night.

Unspoken jokes with each juicy scoop,
Smeared faces in a tiny troop.
Spilling secrets, seeds take flight,
A fruity chorus to our delight.

In every crunch, a tale unfolds,
Of silly antics yet to be told.
With juicy laughter, we unite,
In this fun, our hearts ignite.

The Enchantment of a Juicy Slice

In a garden so bright and sweet,
Melons dance to a summer beat.
With laughter ripe, they tumble down,
Sticky smiles all over the town.

The seeds are like jokes tossed in air,
Each chuckle a splash, oh what a fair!
A juicy grin, a slice so wide,
Fuel for fun, we cannot hide.

Bite into bliss, it's a wacky ride,
With every munch, our worries slide.
The juice dribbles down, a comic sight,
Like chasing rainbows, pure delight.

So gather round, let stories unfold,
Of melons bold and whimsies told.
A carnival of flavor, life's sweet tease,
With every slice, we're sure to please.

Petals and Pulp beneath the Stars

Under the glow of a lunar light,
We feast on slices, hearts so bright.
Petals gather, a fragrant share,
While seeds hop games — oh, what a flare!

Laughter dances on cooling breeze,
As we slurp away, tasting the tease.
A fruit gala laid on canvas sky,
With every bite, we sing and sigh.

The pulp winks at us, what a rogue,
Like cheeky pixies in a green vogue.
Each juicy giggle shared so nice,
Under this fragrant, starry slice.

And when the last bit disappears,
We'll toast with joy, and hearty cheers.
For in this feast, we find our glee,
A night of fun, so wild and free.

Folding Sunlight into Sweetness

Sunlight rolls into our hands,
A sweet creation the summer plans.
With bursts of flavor, it captures the day,
A tango in our tummies, come what may.

Squirrels giggle with cheeky grins,
As we slice and serve, the merriment begins.
Folding sweetness, folding cheer,
With every bite, we forget our fear.

Dripping happiness from every seed,
This fruity joy is all we need.
We play with flavors, toss the rind,
In laughter's whirl, joy intertwined.

As sunshine fades and laughter hums,
We cradle this magic — oh, how it strums!
In every slice, a story bleeds,
Of summer's warmth and playful deeds.

Blossoms of Flavor and Youth

In a patch where dreams take flight,
Little seeds sprout joy, pure delight.
With petals that giggle in the sun,
Each juicy bite is laughter's fun.

Friends gather 'round for a taste parade,
With faces glowing in the shade.
We trade sweet tales and silly winks,
While juicy dribbles lead to pinks.

The crunch of laughter fills the air,
A fruit fiesta, no room for care.
With each slice shared, hearts take bloom,
A garden of flavor, dispelling gloom.

So let's toast to youth, and dance a bit,
In every slice, our spirits fit.
For in this laughter, we find the key,
To blossoms bright, and tastes of glee.

The Garden's Hidden Treats

In the garden, giggles hide,
Where laughter and fruit collide.
A round delight in leafy beds,
Silly jokes dance in our heads.

Beneath the vines, a secret lies,
Green globes with cheeky, grinning eyes.
"Oh look, a treasure!" we sing aloud,
As seeds of joy gather a crowd.

The crunch, the squirt, a juicy cheer,
For fruit so silly, we all draw near.
With every bite, the grins expand,
A fruity party at our command.

Flora of the Fruitful Ground

Among the blooms, a funny sight,
Green helmets roll in pure delight.
"They think they're tough," we laugh and say,
As tiny fruits erupt in play.

The flowers dance, the bees are bold,
Tales of sweetness waiting to be told.
With giggles bouncing on the breeze,
We welcome treats from the trees.

Moments shared in this zany patch,
Whimsy blooms where none can catch.
Nature's joke, we can't ignore,
In the fields where we explore.

A Slice of Summer Spirit

A sunny slice of cheerful sun,
Each bite proves that life is fun.
With seeds on arms like confetti bright,
We laugh until the fall of night.

The juice, it drips, a sweet cascade,
With every chuckle, we just can't fade.
From picnic spreads to garden fairs,
This fruit of laughter brings no cares.

We toss and share, a playful trade,
In warm embrace, no fear nor shade.
Summer's calling, let's all partake,
In this fruity joy, we'll never quake.

Threads of Shade and Sweetness

Under trees, the giggles flow,
As juicy jokes begin to grow.
In chilly shade, we tease and jest,
No silly fruit can outshine the rest.

A slice so bright, it makes us grin,
Silly laughter, let the fun begin!
With sticky fingers and playful sways,
We sip the sunlight on sunny days.

Chasing rays where sweet dreams linger,
Life's a joke, wrapped on a finger.
In every slice, our spirits rise,
As joy-filled laughter fills the skies.

Elysian Fruits at Dusk's Caress

In a garden ripe with delight,
Juicy bites take flight.
A fruit that giggles in the breeze,
Rolling around with such silly ease.

Bright shadows dance on the ground,
As laughter echoes all around.
Chubby cheeks, an inviting sight,
Taste the blush of the summer night.

Nature's candy, sweet and bold,
A tale of laughs waiting to be told.
Slices shared under the moon's glow,
Sun-kissed treasures, come and slow.

In each bite, a burst of fun,
Juicy joy beneath the sun.
Oh, what a dance this treat does prance,
In a fruity, funny, whimsy trance.

Crisp Echoes and Flavorful Whirls

Amidst the crunch and zesty cheer,
A lively hum for all to hear.
With every slice, a giggle formed,
Crisp laughter in flavors warmed.

Golden seeds scatter like dreams,
Crafting joy from summer's beams.
Each bite, a splash of laughter's zest,
Refreshing antics from nature's best.

Little critters join the feast,
Chasing crumbs like a silly beast.
A fruit so bright, it seems to sing,
Inviting all for a sweet fling.

As the sun dips low, we can't resist,
Savoring every glorious twist.
With a crunch and a grin, we play our part,
Sharing love from this juicy heart.

Melon Reflections in Twilight's Embrace

At day's end, a round delight,
Craziness in every bite.
Chilling moments with friends abound,
As laughter dances all around.

Tender hues of orange and green,
A playful snack, oh so keen.
Reflections of joy in the evening glow,
Dancing patterns in a show.

With giggles echoing through the air,
A juicy treat beyond compare.
Cut into triangles, oh what a scene,
Laughter tumbles, bright and keen.

As the twilight hums its tune,
We savor bites beneath the moon.
Nature's joke, a funny affair,
Sweetness bursts, a love we share.

Liquid Sunshine in Every Bite

When midday strikes, a vibrant jest,
A fruity smile, oh how it's best.
Liquid joy from a slip and slide,
Taste the sun, let happiness ride.

A playful splatter on the floor,
Outrageous fun we can't ignore.
With giggles spilling from every spoon,
Creating chaos with a fruity tune.

Splashing and giggling, oh what a sight,
Chasing drips in pure delight.
A sunny treasure, nature's glee,
Every mouthful, a silly spree.

In every scoop, the laughter flows,
Juicy secrets only nature knows.
So grab a slice and take a ride,
To a land where pure joy can't hide.

Harvesting Joy from Nature's Bounty

In fields where the sun tickles the greens,
The round fellows giggle in striped sheens.
Nature's ticklish gift, so plump and bright,
A jolly jester's delight in the light.

Baskets brim full, laughter fills the air,
As juicy treasures tumble without care.
With each sweet bite, a cheer explodes,
In this merry adventure, joy erodes.

Lush Lullabies of the Garden

In the garden where the giggles grow,
Dancing in breezes, they're putting on a show.
Fuzzy green coats, they sway and bow,
Tickling the soil, what a joyful wow!

Each plump orb sings a tale of cheer,
With every munch, all worries disappear.
Garden's melody, a funny refrain,
In each juicy drop, the laughter's plain.

An Ode to the Ripening Season

Oh, season of laughter, how you tease,
With each swell of fruit, it's sure to please.
They plop and roll in a merry parade,
A round festival, in sunlight they played.

The sweet aroma wafts with a spin,
Tickled taste buds, let the fun begin.
As they pop and splatter, giggles ignite,
A tasty comedy, pure delight!.

The Story of an Innocent Slice

Once there was a slice that loved to joke,
With laughter galore, it happily spoke.
It rolled on the table, a merry spree,
Spreading silly rumors, oh could you believe?

Friends would gather, ready to munch,
With juicy giggles at every crunch.
The deed was done, the laughter spread,
Innocence served, with smiles ahead.

The Sweet Call of Summer's Harvest

In fields so bright, a fruit does lie,
Round and green beneath the sky.
With bites so juicy, laughter's cheer,
We'll hold it close, year after year.

The seeds like tiny gems do hide,
In every slice, a summer ride.
We munch and crunch with pure delight,
Under the sun, it's quite a sight!

Oh, sticky hands and faces smeared,
As summer's cheer is truly cleared.
We'll share our bounty, slice by slice,
No room for liars—that's our advice!

So gather 'round, don't lose your place,
With giggles, we will set the pace.
The summer harvest sings a tune,
Of fruit-filled days and nights in June.

Nectarous Dreams Thereby Spread

In dreams of fruit, we sail the sky,
With juicy treats that make us sigh.
A splash of color, green and red,
Adventures wait, just like they said.

Each bite's a burst, a silly dance,
We twirl and spin in fruit's romance.
Juicy dribbles down our chins,
This isn't just a game—we win!

Come take a seat, let's share the fun,
In every slice a story spun.
We laugh at seeds and sticky hands,
While making juicy summer plans.

With visions sweet of goodies bright,
The laughter carries into night.
A nectarous feast we can't resist,
In laughter's glow, we coexist.

Green Caves and Rubies Unveiled

From envious vines, we find the prize,
A treasure hid beneath green skies.
With every slice, the laughter reigns,
As ruby bits break deeper chains.

Hidden caves, oh, so surreal,
We dive right in with our next meal.
The crunch, the squish, a grand parade,
A flavorful mess from what we've made.

Adventure calls, come one, come all,
To taste the magic, big and small.
With giggles echoing all around,
In juicy caves, pure joy is found.

Let's summon forth the seeds of cheer,
With every conquest, summer dear.
We lift our slices to the sky,
In funny feasts, we all comply.

Summer's Celebration of Color

A festival of hues, quite divine,
With reds and greens, we dine in line.
Each bite a giggle, pure and bright,
A summer feast, oh, what a sight!

From picnic mats, we rule the show,
With juicy smiles, our laughter flows.
The squishy texture, oh, so grand,
In every corner, sticky hand!

Let's toast to losses of our woes,
With every slice, our joy just grows.
The vibrant banquet, nature's gift,
In every bite, our spirits lift.

So break the slice; our team's complete,
In laughter's play, we find our beat.
With colors dancing on the tongue,
Our summer anthem's been well sung!

Juicy Secrets of Summer

In the sun, a treasure waits,
Red and green, it celebrates.
Biting in, the juice does flow,
Sticky fingers, don't you know?

Giggles shared with every bite,
Silly seeds take wing in flight.
Slurping sounds, the laughter rings,
Who knew fruit could have such things?

Echoes Beneath the Rind

Hidden tales in every slice,
A fruity life, a cool paradise.
With each crunch, a story told,
Adventures ripe, and fun unfolds.

Seeds embark on journeys wild,
As laughter bursts, we're all like children.
Underneath the summer sun,
The freshest fun has just begun.

Serenade of Slices

Summer's breeze and juicy bites,
Dancing slices, pure delights.
Singing tunes, the juice does flow,
Melon songs, never slow.

Chillin' out with fruity cheer,
No worries here, just laughter near.
Each juicy piece a melody,
Slicing up a symphony.

Melon Murmurs at Dusk

As the sun begins to dip,
We snack and giggle, take a sip.
Glimmers of pink in the fading light,
Melon fun on this warm night.

Crickets join our joyful feast,
Their serenade, a blissful beast.
With every slice, the laughter spills,
Even dusk can't quiet our thrills.

A Symphony of Seeds and Sweets

On a picnic rug, we lay,
Laughter mingles with the day.
Juicy bites, a sticky mess,
Seeds spitting—oh, what a stress!

With every slice, a story shared,
Sticky fingers, none prepared.
Giggles rising with each taste,
A bait for bees, it's quite the waste!

The drippy juice, a summer treat,
Ants march in, we face defeat.
But in the chaos, joy prevails,
As laughter dances in the trails!

In shades of green, the fruit's delight,
A funny feast that feels just right.
With every bite, our troubles flee,
This silly snack's a jubilee!

The Art of Savoring Delights

A slice of red, a burst of cheer,
Making friends from far and near.
Juice dripping off our chins like rain,
We find sweet bliss among the grain!

The battle starts, it's every seed,
Flinging bits—it's not too sweet!
With messy hands and happy sighs,
We toast the summer, watch it rise!

Tickling tongues, a flavor fest,
Who knew this fruit would be the best?
In every wedge, a secret's spun,
A comedy of snacks, oh, what fun!

So here's to joy and juicy treats,
The art of bites, oh, how it beats!
Savoring laughter, amidst the fun,
In each sweet moment, we are one!

Reflections in a Melon's Heart

A melon meets the sunny sky,
It smiles down, oh my, oh my!
With a grin so wide, it gleams,
Chasing away our silly dreams.

We dive in deep, a juicy plunge,
Amidst the seeds, we start to lunge.
Belly laughs, oh what a sight,
A fruit-filled brawl, a pure delight!

In every chunk, a giggle found,
As laughter echoes all around.
With playful bites, we snack and share,
A fruity gala, oh, how rare!

Reflections dance in every drop,
This silly fun, it can't be stopped.
So let's embrace this playful art,
The joy we find, a melting heart!

The Linger of Summer's Taste

The sun spills gold on every slice,
A carnival of flavor—oh so nice!
Chomp and chew, a cheerful fight,
Each bite ignites our taste buds' light!

In laughter's wake, we find our groove,
Sliding seeds like a silly move.
Slipping on rinds, we take a fall,
But giggles rise to conquer all!

Threads of sweetness through our days,
Sticky moments in so many ways.
With cheeks stained crimson, we parade,
In this funny feast, memories are made!

So here's to bites that make us sway,
In summer's linger, come what may.
We'll savor joy in fruity bliss,
A quirky touch we can't dismiss!

Ethereal Threads of Flavor

In a patch of green, a fruit does bounce,
With seeds that giggle, oh what a pounce!
Pink juice drips down, like a silly show,
Munching and crunching, let the good times flow.

Sticky fingers wave, in delight and glee,
A juicy jester, how could it be?
The laughter rises, with every bite,
This fruity prankster, a pure delight!

Oh, summer's jest, in each bite so bold,
A tale of sweetness, at least tenfold.
Nature's comedy, on picnic days,
With giggling friends, in sunny rays.

So grab a slice, let joy parade,
In every crumble, let memories fade.
With every slurp, and chuckle loud,
Dance with the fruit, in laughter's cloud.

A Summer's Borealis in a Bowl

A bowl of joy, bright and round,
Colors collide, the flavors abound.
Red and green, a playful fight,
This fruity delight, pure summer's light.

Sunshine breaks as giggles rise,
Each juicy bite, a sweet surprise.
With every slice, a tasty tease,
Nature's punchline, sure to please.

Chilling in ice, like a cool breeze,
A pool of laughter, that aims to please.
Sippers and slurpers, join the show,
In a fruity swirl, let's blow and blow!

As laughter echoes, and juice does flow,
Who knew a bowl could steal the show?
A festival of taste, in every scoop,
Under the sun, we all come loop.

Garden Whispers in a Crimson Glow

In hidden gardens, secrets bloom,
A crimson orb, banish your gloom.
Silly giggles when it's revealed,
This quirky fruit, a joy fielded.

Sliced and served, it wobbles round,
Each juicy bite, a giggly sound.
Seeds like confetti, fly through the air,
A party in summer, without a care.

With sticky lips, we share a grin,
Every bite's a cheeky win.
Crimson drama in every slice,
Laughter spun, with fruity nice!

So grab a fork, let's make a mess,
In this fruity joy, we all digress.
Nature's chuckle, in every bite,
Living the dream, in summer's light.

The Harmony of Green and Gold

Green on the outside, gold within,
A fruit so sly, let the fun begin.
Chomping joyously, can you believe,
This merry treat, you won't want to leave!

A party on tongues, flavors collide,
Frustration's forgotten with each juicy slide.
Squirts of sunshine, laughter ignites,
As we dive into fruity delights.

Picnic blankets, laughter flows wide,
With each tossed slice, hearts open wide.
Green and gold, a duo so bold,
Frivolous giggles, stories retold.

So lift your forks, join in the cheer,
With this fruity charm, there's nothing to fear.
It's a dance of flavors, a carnival spree,
In the land of joy, fruity jubilee!

The Rhythms of a Summer Feast

Juicy bites, oh what a treat,
Laughter bursts at every seat.
Seeds fly high with every cheer,
Sticky fingers, summer's near.

Giggles dance like fireflies,
As we crunch beneath the skies.
Peel the rind, let laughter flow,
A fruity feast, let good times grow.

Picnic spreads like painter's art,
Squina's juice, it plays its part.
Everyone grabs a sloppy slice,
Feasting here is oh-so-nice!

From the red to bright green rind,
In this joy, we all unwind.
Tummy aches from too much fun,
Underneath the golden sun.

Beneath the Crescent Moon's Gaze

Moonlit glow on summer nights,
Fruit-filled laughter, such delights.
Chasing shadows, kids do sing,
While the stars join in, they swing.

Sticky steps on lawn so green,
What a sight, a silly scene!
Stern-faced adults now partake,
In the fun, they can't forsake.

Melodies of giggles loud,
In this gathering, we feel proud.
A mist of sweetness fills the air,
And half the juice ends up in hair.

Nights roll on with happy cheer,
As each slice brings joy so near.
In the moon's soft, glowing light,
Every one smiles, pure delight.

Slices of Summer's Song

Beneath the shade, the fun begins,
With each slice, everyone grins.
A rhythm of laughter fills the space,
Juicy joy, let's to embrace.

Chomping down with no regret,
Messy faces, no need to fret.
Kids are giggling, oh so loud,
While parents share a laughter cloud.

A dance of flavors, sweet and bright,
Spinning tales in summer light.
People gathering, sharing glee,
Slices like treasures, wild and free.

With each bite, the good times flow,
On this adventure, let's all go!
Every slice a little song,
In this moment, we belong.

Tranquil Tides at Twilight's Edge

Evening calm, a slice in hand,
Giggling, we stroll on the sand.
Rippling waves sing to the shore,
Where fruity tales wait to explore.

Summer breezes gently tease,
As we munch with joyful ease.
Splashes of color, rinds laid bare,
Sipping nectar, without a care.

Time slows down in twilight's grace,
On this beach, life's a big race.
With laughter echoing all around,
In sweet moments of joy, we're bound.

At dusk's embrace, we all concede,
Life is best with fruity feed.
As day fades into night's song,
In these flavors, we belong.

Chants of the Crimson Heart

In fields of green, they gather round,
To praise the fruit that rolls on ground.
With stripes of joy, they dance and cheer,
A giggle here, a slice of cheer!

The seeds like jewels, they spit with glee,
A spitty game, pure jubilee.
The juice that drips, a sticky mess,
Oh what a thrill, what pure excess!

From picnic baskets, joy does soar,
Laughter lifts, they ask for more.
A fruit so bold, both sweet and stout,
In summer's heat, we scream and shout!

So gather friends, let fun commence,
In every slice lies pure suspense.
The crimson heart, our festive muse,
In playful bites, we cannot lose!

Poems from the Patch

From fields of green, with sun in sight,
A fruit parade, a sheer delight.
They tumble down, oh what a race,
We roll and laugh, in this sweet place!

The patch is loud, with giggles bright,
As juicy bites bring pure delight.
We stab our forks, our aims are poor,
Who made that mess? Oh, what a chore!

With every drip, a race begins,
To see who spills, and who just grins.
It's chaos here, but all in fun,
We're under the sun, we've just begun!

In every bite, there's joy to find,
In laughter shared, we're intertwined.
The patch our stage, for all to see,
A fruity show, how sweet we be!

Forbidden Fruit's Lullaby

A fruit so red, with secrets held,
In gardens lush, where laughter swelled.
Sneaky bites, behind the fence,
It's pure delight, and recompense!

In shadows deep, we slice and share,
Forbidden treats, with naught a care.
A giggle bursts, oh what a thrill,
The juice that stains, we feel it still!

With every seed, a story grows,
Of fun and games, of summer's shows.
We can't resist the juicy bliss,
A stolen slice, oh do you miss?

So hush, dear friends, let laughter flow,
In secret spots, our joy will grow.
The fruits of summer, bold and bright,
In playful hearts, we find our light!

Summer's Sweetest Confessions

Oh juicy tales, we love to share,
With sticky hands and fruity hair.
We gather close, the sun ablaze,
In warm embrace, we spend our days.

Confessions made with every bite,
Of favorite fruit and pure delight.
We spill our dreams with every seed,
Unplugged from worries, it's all we need!

With laughter ringing, hearts set free,
We dance around with jubilee.
A playful fight, who gets the last?
We laugh and cheer, forget the past!

So here's to days of juicy joy,
No need for fancy, just little toys.
In summer's glow, where spirits blend,
Our sweetest tales will never end!

Enchanted Melodies of the Melon

A ball of green, so round and bright,
Its pinky insides, a joyful sight.
Slice it open, hear the cheer,
Seeds go flying, oh dear, oh dear!

Juicy laughter, sticky hands,
We giggle, running 'cross the sands.
Each tasty bite, a drippy splat,
Who knew fruit could cause such chat?

Friends gather close, the picnic's grand,
Juice dribbles down, a lively band.
With every crunch, another joke,
In the heat, our laughter spoke.

Let's dance around this sweet delight,
In the summer sun, everything's right.
A melon's magic, a slice of play,
Creating smiles that will stay!

Revelations of Summer's Heart

Bright and juicy, a summer prize,
Laughter echoes, under blue skies.
Biting through this crimson bliss,
Who can resist a melon's kiss?

Pitch perfect flavor, it's quite a hit,
With sticky hands, we never quit.
A fruit so grand, it makes us dance,
In juicy joy, we take a chance.

It rolls away, our silly game,
Chasing after, calling its name.
Silly antics, all in good fun,
Melon moments, two for one!

So grab a slice and hold it tight,
Dare to share in this delight.
As laughter echoes, let's take hold,
Of sweet memories, pure as gold!

Lush Melodies of Seasons Past

As summer wanes, we take a bite,
A melody of flavors, pure delight.
Slides with a splash, a fruity song,
In every crunch, we can't go wrong!

Nibbles shared beneath the trees,
We giggle softly with the breeze.
A splash of juice, a sticky face,
In our hearts, this playful space.

Friends join round, with spoons in hand,
Sipping sweetness, oh, it's grand!
Laughter twinkles, as we compete,
For the last bite of this tasty treat.

Memories made with every chew,
Mirth flows freely, it's something new.
Dance, laugh, and let the fun grow,
With every slice, our spirits glow!

Taste of the Afternoon Sun

A summer treat, all cold and sweet,
In every slice, laughter's heartbeat.
Playing tricks with juice and seeds,
We plant delight, and joy proceeds.

Bite-sized giggles, the sun's warm kiss,
Rolling laughter, nothing's amiss.
We toss it high, like a game of catch,
Calling the neighbors, 'Oh, here's the catch!'

Sunburned noses and smiles so wide,
Sipping sweetness, our hearts fill with pride.
Listen closely, the fruit's a rhyme,
In every moment, it's summer time!

So let's savor this fruity show,
With every slice, our warmth will grow.
Let's laugh, crunch, and share our fun,
This sunny joy has just begun!

Sweet Sorrows in Pink

In the bowl, they sit and grin,
Wobbly slices wearing a skin.
Juicy secrets dripping down,
No one wears a frowning crown.

Bites taken, giggles shared,
Sticky fingers, hearts prepared.
Laughter spills like a sweet drink,
Who knew fruit could make you think?

Melon dreams on summer days,
Sipping juice in funny ways.
Maybe it's the seeds we spit,
Or the puns that never quit.

In the end, we munch and sigh,
Eating pink till we comply.
Sweet sorrows in each bright bite,
Dancing in the warm moonlight.

Beneath the Green Veil

Under leaves, a treasure found,
Giggles echo all around.
In the patch, they play a game,
Each one thinking they're the same.

Seeds like marbles, crazy fun,
Tossing them, we try to run.
A sticky race, who's the best?
Winning crowns with no contest.

Pink and green do tango sweet,
Melon slices, summer's treat.
Voices rise, the flavor's right,
Laughter sprinkles through the night.

Beneath the veil of leafy twirls,
Joyful chaos, sweet curls.
Funny faces, silly sounds,
With each slice, pure joy abounds.

Laughter from the Orchard

In the orchard, fruits collide,
Juicy giggles, we can't hide.
Water runs, a merry race,
Pink delight splashed on our face.

Rolling past, an awkward trip,
Fruit flies dance around our lips.
Each silly slip a toast to cheer,
Messy friends are always near.

Seeds are flying, what a sight!
Like little missiles in our flight.
Cracking jokes with fruity flare,
In this orchard, laughter's rare.

Squeezed out juice, a brave new scheme,
We laugh and dance, a juicy dream.
With every bite, the fun expands,
Creating joys with sticky hands.

Reflections on a Juicy Dream

In the sun, reflections shine,
A juicy treasure, simply divine.
Pink droplets spark like stars at night,
Each taste a giggle, pure delight.

Dipping fingers, taking licks,
Summer bliss in fruity tricks.
Dancing flavors, can't resist,
Memories wrapped in juicy mist.

Laughter's echo, sweet refrain,
Melon mischief we contain.
Grab a slice, let's take a leap,
In this dream, the joy runs deep.

Under shade, we find a tune,
Singing soft to the warm afternoon.
Reflections bright, we laugh and beam,
Lost together in this dream.

Tales of the Sun-Kissed Harvest

In fields of green, where laughter grows,
Sun-kissed fruits hide, in rows they pose.
Giggles erupt from a juicy surprise,
As sticky sweet juice drips from our eyes.

A seedy debate, who's the winner today?
The one with the biggest slice, hooray!
Fingers all sticky, but spirits so high,
With each silly bite, we can't help but sigh.

The picnic's a riot, the ants join the game,
Cucumber jealousy, they all are to blame.
We toss them the scraps while we snack and play,
Leaving our worries to melt right away.

So bring on the laughter, the sunshine, the fun,
From sun-kissed crops, there's joy for everyone.
With every round bite, our giggles expand,
A feast of good times, so perfectly planned.

Magic Hidden in a Rind

A round, green fortress hides treasure inside,
With stripes like a plane, oh what a ride!
Crack it wide open, let sweetness pour out,
Who knew such delight could cause such a shout?

Our mouths turn to smiles, each slice brings a cheer,
Synchronized laughter with each juicy smear.
Seeds on our faces, we're champions today,
Creating a mess in the best kind of way.

Tickling our tongues with flavors so bright,
Never knew munching could feel this right.
Silliness reigns, as we share in the fun,
All thanks to the magic that shines from the sun.

Cheers to this feast, a sweet summer fling,
With giggles and grins, let the good times swing.
In every bright bite, joy does abound,
In the kingdom of fruits, we're lost and found.

The Texture of Summertime Glow

A canvas of green with a rosy delight,
Beneath the sun's gaze, everything feels right.
Slicing into summer, with crunch to the core,
Sunshine is sparkled, we keep wanting more.

Joy sprinkled high with each playful bite,
We laugh as it dribbles, oh what a sight!
Each bit brings a story, a chuckle or two,
Sticky, sweet moments, a mouthful to chew.

The flavor's contagious, like giggles they spread,
Adventure in every slice, laughter ahead.
Friends gather 'round as the sun starts to set,
Painting our memories, best times yet met.

With juice on our cheeks and smiles all aglow,
In the simple act of munching, we grow.
So here's to the taste, the texture, the show,
In summertime's circle, delight ever flows.

Secrets Buried in Green Shelters

In a patch of green, secrets lay undisclosed,
With a jolly surprise lurking, nobody knows.
Dig deep to uncover these wonders so grand,
And laughter erupts like a joy-filled band.

A slice for a smile, seeds flying with glee,
Who knew such a treat could be wild and free?
With every soft bite, we dance in delight,
As the sun starts to fade, making magic tonight.

Covered in giggles, no care in the world,
As friends share the bounty, the joy is unfurled.
From fridge to the table, the fun's just begun,
Behind every green cloak, shines warmth from the sun.

So lift up your plates, let's toast to the cheer,
Where laughter is loud, and the taste is sincere.
In bites of the juicy, we find our true kin,
Through the secrets we share, the fun will begin.

Emerald Shadows and Ruby Glow

In summer's laughter, bright and bold,
A tale unfolds, or so I'm told.
Green stripes dance on a juicy sphere,
Biting delights bring everyone cheer.

Juicy laughter spills down our chins,
Sticky fingers, where fun begins.
Friends gather 'round with wide-spread glee,
As the gem of summer sets us free.

With every slice, a giggle bursts,
As seeds fly like confetti, no one thirsts.
Mouths agape in sheer delight,
This fruity fest shines so bright.

Emerald shadows play in the sun,
Ruby globes promise tasty fun.
A summer troop, with laughter, we flow,
In this fruity feast, all worries go.

Dappled Light on Juicy Horizons

A playground made of pink and green,
Where munchers gather, a vibrant scene.
Sunny spots where giggles ignite,
As juicy treasures take their flight.

The crunch of bites echoes in air,
Sticky smiles, no one can compare.
Dappled light plays tricks on our eyes,
As laughter erupts with each surprise.

Rainbow seeds scattered on the ground,
In this escapade, joy is found.
With shades of summer, we all partake,
In this silly game, we laugh and shake.

Juicy horizons call us near,
Under bright skies, dancing with cheer.
In every slice, a memory sticks,
Laughter rings with every kick.

Secrets Held in a Sundrenched Fruit

Beneath the sun's warm, playful gaze,
Secrets burst, like a summer phase.
A fruit of joy, vibrant and sweet,
In this orchard, happiness meets.

Tiny seeds in a cheeky race,
Splattered juice, our silly face.
With every laugh, the stories grow,
In one big bite, our spirits glow.

We stash our worries in grassy nooks,
Trading them for juicy looks.
With playful grins, we take a seat,
Fruity treasures, oh, what a treat!

Secrets held in every slice,
Life's little giggles, oh so nice.
With each sunbeam, our spirits zoom,
In this silly feast, there's plenty of room.

Sun-Kissed Revelations

Under sun-kissed rays, we gather 'round,
Where fruity treasures, laughter abound.
Juicy slices, a vibrant show,
In every grin, summer's glow.

As we munch on bright delights,
Tickled toes on balmy nights.
Juicy secrets in every bite,
Making moments feel just right.

Fruits tickle our taste buds' core,
With sprightly games and playful lore.
Laughter dances through the air,
In this sweet world, we have no care.

Sun-kissed revelations, sweet and bold,
In this playful tale, joy unfolds.
With every nibble and every cheer,
Summer's delight is always near.

Voices from the Fruit Stand

In the bright sun, a melon grins,
Telling tales of juicy sins.
Laughter rises, seeds take flight,
A fruity joke born from delight.

A green round ball, full of cheer,
One bite in, it's clear, oh dear!
Squirty fun, juice everywhere,
Summer's joy, without a care.

Chubby slices laugh and dance,
Slice me up, give taste a chance!
Giggles bubble from the rind,
Delicious chaos, oh so kind!

Under the sun, they play their tune,
A fruity feast, oh, what a boon!
With every crunch, a giggle spills,
Nature's humor; oh, what thrills!

Vibrations of a Sweet Slice

In sun-soaked fields, sweet slices sing,
Jokesters dressed in green, they swing.
On plates they land, they boast their charms,
With sticky hands and happy arms.

Laughter erupts as juice drips down,
Making faces, turning into clowns.
Silly seeds dance in a row,
Who knew fruit could steal the show?

Each bite's a giggle, rich and deep,
Melon magic makes us leap.
Tasting joy, we all convene,
Fruity shenanigans, so serene!

So grab a slice, don't be late,
Join the laughter on your plate.
In every nibble, joy resides,
Where fruit and fun can't be denied!

Serenading the Summer Sun

On sunny days, the fruit parade,
Melon slices, ready-made.
Singing sweet, a juicy song,
Summer's delight, where we belong.

A chill bite shouts, 'Come on, friends!'
Juicy humor never ends.
With each chuckle, seeds take flight,
Bright and cheerful, pure delight!

Ballooning bellies, laughter wide,
Glorious madness, side by side.
As sunshine warms the picnic place,
Melon tales put smiles on the face.

So gather 'round, feast upon,
Nature's jest till daylight's gone!
Let your worries drift away,
Join the fruit fiesta, hooray!

Breath of the Garden's Joy

In the garden, colors cheer,
Melon chortles, drawing near.
Sassy vines tell goofy tales,
With giggling leaves and playful gales.

A slice of joy, a splash of fun,
Underneath the warming sun.
Seeds take bets on who can roll,
A fruity race, let's lose control!

Chanting greens and reds collide,
With juicy secrets, they abide.
One tiny bite brings big delight,
Fruity chuckles take to flight!

Nature's humor fills the air,
Messy hands show we don't care.
In every slice, a taste of glee,
Fruit's sweet laughter, wild and free!

The Secret Life of a Summer Harvest

In the garden, tales abound,
Cucumbers gossip, melons clown.
Tomatoes tickle, peppers laugh,
Roots dance below, their secret path.

Rheumy radishes tell their jokes,
While leafy greens play pranks on folks.
Pumpkins roll with glee at night,
Under the moon, it's quite a sight.

On one funny day, they all conspire,
To launch a fruit parade—oh, they're quite the choir!
Chanting rhythms of summer's cheer,
While ants march along, holding beers.

They plot the harvest with funny flair,
Winking at humans, unaware.
As farmers toil and sweat, they squirm,
Knowing the jokes are theirs to affirm.

Harmony in Every Drip.

A squirt of juice, a splash of fun,
Bouncing berries, all on the run.
Drips of nectar and seeds galore,
Nature's laugh is hard to ignore.

Water drops dance on leaves so green,
A slippery show, a comedic scene.
Lemons crack jokes while limes just giggle,
As apples chuckle, doing a wiggle.

Each drop like a note in a playful song,
Singing softly, where fruits belong.
Bees tap their feet, they join the groove,
In a sticky rhythm, they all move.

As rain taps down, the party starts,
Roots sway to the beats, sharing hearts.
No fruit too shy, no vein too rickety,
In this orchard, life is always tricky!

Juicy Secrets of a Summer's Fruit

In shades of red and neon green,
Fruits conspire in a clever scene.
Basketball berries bounce in delight,
Sharing their secrets in summer's light.

Bananas plot with witty ease,
Peeking at pears like playful tease.
Oranges chuckle, rolling round,
Spreading joy with citrus sounds.

Each slice reveals a juicy tale,
Of summer sun and breezy sail.
A mango's giggle is hard to bite,
As passionfruit whispers of love at night.

Ripe grapes gossip in a tangled vine,
While cherries play games, crossing the line.
Every fruit has a story felt,
And in their laughter, summer's heart melts.

Echoes of Sweetness in the Orchard

In the orchard, sweet sounds collide,
Where fruits find humor in the wide.
A cantaloupe roars with a hearty cheer,
While berries snicker, "Is that a deer?"

Peaches rolled off in a giggly spree,
With plums tagging along, wild and free.
The air is filled with joyful cries,
As pineapples sport their spiky ties.

Leaves rustle softly, making a fuss,
While the sun laughs, no need to rush.
Fruits play tricks on the farmer's hat,
Dropping down while he's busy and flat.

When harvest comes, they're full of glee,
Creating chaos, then disappearing spree.
In every bite, laughter's found,
As sweetness echoes all around.

Nectar from the Garden

In a patch where the bright fruits grow,
Chubby cheeks munching, oh what a show!
Juices running down, a sticky delight,
Sunshine giggles on a warm, silly night.

Leaves rustle softly, a playful tune,
Bumblebees buzzing 'neath the light of the moon.
Squirrels plotting mischief in every vine,
As we laugh at the spills of sweet, purple brine.

Tiny seeds fly through the air with glee,
Hoping to land on a branch of a tree.
Gardener's frown as the critters take flight,
While we feast on sweetness—a pure, cheeky bite.

What joy we find in the patch's embrace,
As we dance 'round puddles, with watermelon grace.
With every bite shared, laughter ignites,
In the garden's bright love, everything feels right.

Sun-Kissed Memories

Under the sun, we flop down and sigh,
Slicing the fruit, it's the star of the sky.
Its pinky interior, a giggle machine,
Juicy shenanigans, a past summer scene.

Friends wearing hats, with laughter like cheer,
As sticky juice drips—the best souvenir.
Ants start to march, all lined up in rows,
Sharing the feast, it's a humorous pose.

Count the sweet bites, as we laugh and explore,
My shirt's now a canvas, oh, what a chore!
But who needs clean when there's joy to uphold?
Sunshine and laughter, a story retold.

Let's raise a toast to the fruit of the day,
With each silly slip, we'll giggle and play.
Memories made under wide-open skies,
In sun-kissed moments, love never dies.

The Hidden Taste of Delight

Sneaking a slice, oh what a surprise,
It's a juicy treasure that opens our eyes.
Playing with flavors while making a mess,
The hidden sweet gems, we surely bless.

A sprinkle of salt, just for some flair,
Neighbors peeking over, caught in our affair.
Laughter erupts like bubbles in air,
As we share the goodies without a care.

The look on your face, when you bite in deep,
Knowing full well, it just might make you weep.
But laughter ends up as the best kind of balm,
With each sticky moment, the vibe stays calm.

So slice it up quick, let the fun begin,
With sticky fingers, there's no trace of sin.
We'll dance in the sweetness, no need to be coy,
In this delightful moment, let's spread the joy.

Glistening Graces of July

When July arrives, the laughter ignites,
With fruit in our hands, oh what silly sights!
Watermelon laughter, rolling like a ball,
As juice drips and splashes, oh what a sprawl!

Sneaking a bite while dodging the seeds,
With friends all around, fulfilling our needs.
Games of giant slices, who takes the crown?
Whoever takes the biggest, deserves the renown!

Underneath the sun's gaze, we're all in a race,
To devour the sweetness without any grace.
Laughter mixes with juice, a slippery flair,
As the critters gather, frantically aware.

So here's to July, with its giggles galore,
Where every bite brings out shouts for more.
In the glistening fun, with joy fixed in sight,
We'll savor each moment, our hearts feeling light.

www.ingramcontent.com/pod-product-compliance
Lightning Source LLC
Chambersburg PA
CBHW051733290426
43661CB00123B/257